DISCOVER SCIENCE

MOUNTAINS

KINGFISHER

Published in 2012 by Kingfisher
This edition published 2017 by Kingfisher
an imprint of Macmillan Children's Books
20 New Wharf Road, London N1 9RR
Associated companies throughout the world
www.panmacmillan.com

ISBN 978-0-7534-4147-3

First published as Kingfisher Young Knowledge: Mountains in 2007
Additional material produced for Macmillan Children's Books by Discovery Books Ltd
Cover design by Wildpixel Ltd

3 5 7 9 8 6 4 2
2TR/0517/UTD/WKT/128MA

A CIP catalogue record for this book is available from the British Library.

Printed in China

Note to readers: the website addresses listed in this book are correct at the time of going to print.
However, due to the ever-changing nature of the internet, website addresses and content can
change. Websites can contain links that are unsuitable for children. The publisher cannot be held responsible
for changes in website addresses or content, or for information obtained through
a third party. We strongly advise that internet searches be supervised by an adult.

Acknowledgements
The publisher would like to thank the following for permission to reproduce their material.
b = bottom, c = centre, l = left, t = top, r = right

Photographs: cover all images courtesy of Shutterstock; Page 1 Corbis/W Wayne Lockwood; 2–3 Corbis/
Charlie Munsey; 4–5 Alamy/Nagelestock; 6–7 Corbis/Eye Ubiquitous; 7tr Corbis/Galen Rowell; 9 Shutterstock/
fpolat; 10–11 iStock/Salvov; 11br Getty/Science Faction; 12 Corbis/Joseph Sohm; 13 Corbis/Ric Ergenbright;
15tr Frank Lane Picture Agency/Winfried Wisniewski; 15bl iStock/bibikoff; 16–17 Getty/Stone; 17br Alamy/Aflo
Foto; 18l Corbis/Galen Rowell; 18–19 Getty/Imagebank; 19r Getty/Dave Porter Peterborough UK; 20 Corbis/
Eye Ubiquitous;21t Corbis/Tom Bean; 21br Corbis/Paul A Souders; 22 Alamy/Brett Baunton; 23t Natural
History Picture Agency/Alberto Nardi; 23b Science Photo Library/Kaj R Svensson; 24 Corbis/Steve Kaufman;
25t iStock/PaulTessier; 25b Corbis/Joe McDonald; 26c Alamy/Andrew Woodley; 26–27b Getty/Stone;
27t Alamy/Terry Fincher Photos; 28–29 Getty/David Beaty/Robert Harding; 29t Alamy/Mediacolor's;
30 Corbis/Zefa; 31t iStock/sportstock; 31br Alamy/Leon Werdinger; 32 Getty/Digital Vision; 33tl Alamy/David
R Frazier Photolibrary; 33b Alamy/Phototake; 34 Alamy/Publiphoto Diffusion; 35tl John Cleare Mountain
Camera; 35b Getty/Photographer's Choice; 36c Alamy/Pictorial Press Ltd; 36br Alamy/RealyEasyStar/Mark
Edward Smith; 37 Rex Features/Sipa Press; 38 Alamy/f1 online; 38–39 Alamy/StockShot; 39c Corbis/Ashley
Cooper; 40 Corbis/EPA; 41t Corbis/John van Hasselt; 41b iStock/atref; 43tl Getty/NGS; 43b Mary Evans
Picture Library; 48 Shutterstock/Ricardo Manuel Silva de Sousa; 49t Shutterstock/steve100; 49b Shutterstock/
Galyna Andrushko; 52 Shutterstock/Sam D Cruz; 53bl Shutterstock /Luigi Nifosi; 53br Shutterstock/Vulkanette;
56 Shutterstock/hipproductions.

Illustrations on pages: 8, 11, 12, 13, 16 Peter Winfield; 14–15 Steve Weston
Commissioned photography on pages 44–47 by Andy Crawford
Thank you to models Jamie Chang-Leng, Mary Conquest and Georgina Page

MOUNTAINS

Margaret Hynes

KINGFISHER

Contents

What are mountains?

A mountain is a giant, steep-sided rock that rises above the Earth's surface. There are mountains on land, under the oceans and even on other planets.

Mighty mountain ranges

A group of mountains is called a range. The Himalayas is a mountain range in Asia. It is home to the world's highest peaks.

Cold at the top

There is less, or thinner, air at the top of a mountain than there is at the bottom. It is also colder, so some peaks are snowy all year round.

Moving world

The Earth's rocky surface is called the crust. It is divided into plates, which fit together like a jigsaw. The plates move very slowly over the face of the Earth.

Moving plates

This map shows the plates and the direction they are moving in. Some plates crash into each other, while others pull apart.

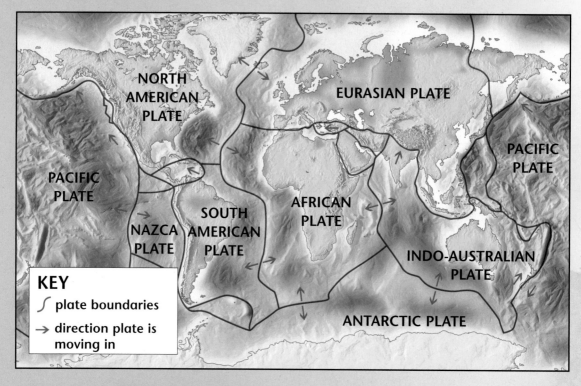

NORTH AMERICAN PLATE

EURASIAN PLATE

PACIFIC PLATE

PACIFIC PLATE

AFRICAN PLATE

NAZCA PLATE

SOUTH AMERICAN PLATE

INDO-AUSTRALIAN PLATE

ANTARCTIC PLATE

KEY
∫ plate boundaries
→ direction plate is moving in

Earthquakes

When the edges of two plates grip each other, the plates cannot move. If they shift suddenly, an earthquake happens, causing terrible damage.

Mountains of fire

Some mountains are volcanoes. They form when hot, melted rock, called magma, erupts from a crack in the Earth's crust. The liquid rock cools and hardens into a mountain.

Violent eruption

Mount Etna is a volcano in Italy. When it erupts, magma bursts out. Ash, gas, steam and hot rocks shoot into the sky.

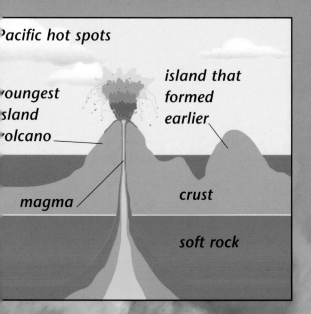

Pacific hot spots

youngest
island
volcano

magma

island that
formed
earlier

crust

soft rock

Hot spots

The Hawaiian
islands are volcanoes.
They form as the Pacific
plate passes over a hot
and active area under
the Earth's crust called
a hot spot.

Flowing lava

Once magma pours out
of a volcano, it is called
lava. It rolls downhill,
like a river of fire.

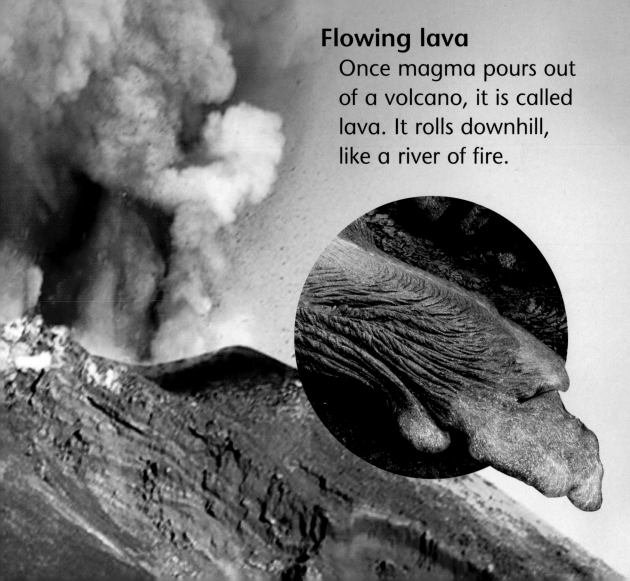

Rising rock

Many mountains form in areas where plates push against each other. The moving plates squeeze the land up, creating mountains.

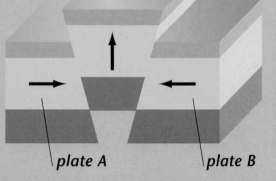

squeezing action push up blocks of rock

plate A *plate B*

Fault-block mountains

The moving plates can cause cracks in the crust. These break the crust into blocks and some rise up to form fault-block mountains.

Rounded off

The Wasatch range in Utah, USA, is a fault-block mountain range. Its blocky shape has been worn down over time.

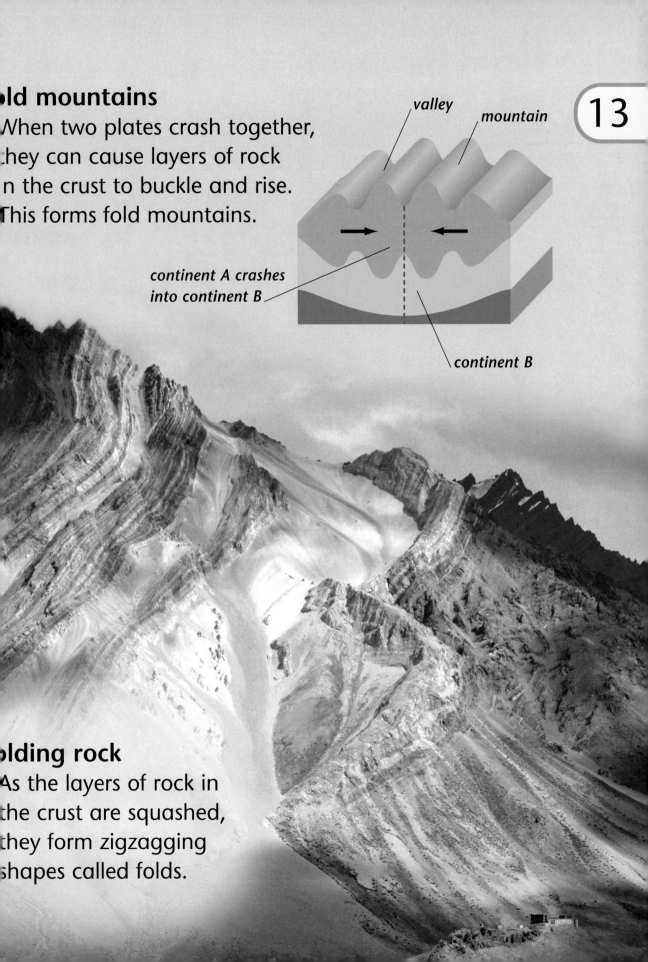

Fold mountains

When two plates crash together, they can cause layers of rock in the crust to buckle and rise. This forms fold mountains.

valley

mountain

continent A crashes into continent B

continent B

Folding rock

As the layers of rock in the crust are squashed, they form zigzagging shapes called folds.

On the mountainsid

A high mountain has several zones, or regions. Each zone has different plants and animals. Very few plants or animals live near the top.

Plant cover

    Forests cover the mountain's lower region. Further up is a zone of small, low-lying plants called alpines.

conifers

deciduous trees

icy peak _____

alpine region

Mountain birds

The wind is so strong at the top of mountains that only powerful birds, such as this lammergeier, can fly there.

Conifers

These cones and pine needles belong to the spruce conifer. Conifer trees have a triangular shape. This helps the snow to slide off them.

Mountain weather

The weather can change very quickly on mountains. A storm can start in just a few minutes. The temperature can quickly drop to below freezing.

Rain shelter

Some mountains are so high they block rain clouds. One slope may be rainy while the other side stays dry.

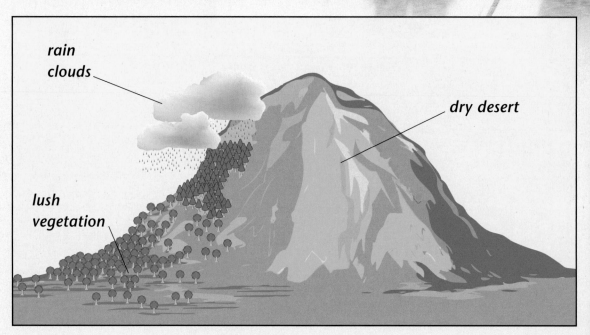

rain clouds

dry desert

lush vegetation

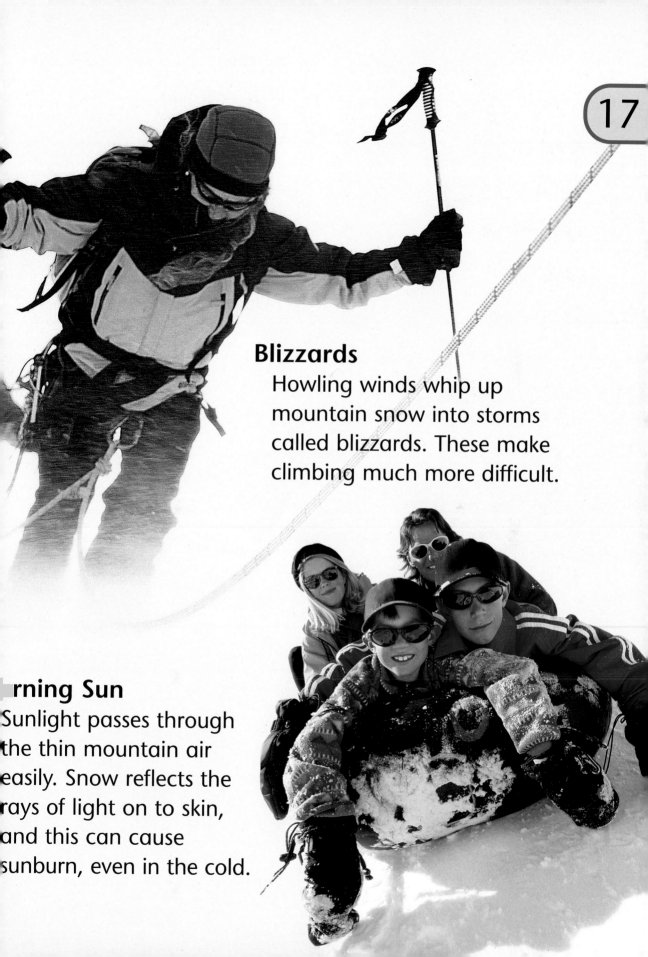

Blizzards

Howling winds whip up mountain snow into storms called blizzards. These make climbing much more difficult.

rning Sun

Sunlight passes through the thin mountain air easily. Snow reflects the rays of light on to skin, and this can cause sunburn, even in the cold.

Glaciers

Great rivers of ice, called glaciers, form on the peaks of some of the world's highest mountains. The glaciers move downhill very slowly.

How glaciers form

Snow collects in rocky hollows, called cirques, high up the mountain. The snow turns into ice, and forms a glacier.

Cracks in the ice

Cracks, called crevasses, form
in a glacier as it moves over
bumpy ground. They are
very deep and dangerous
so climbers use safety ropes.

Left behind

Glaciers pick up rubble and
drag it along with them.
When the ice melts, these
rocks are left behind.

Wear and tear

All mountains are under attack from the elements. Ice, wind and running water slowly wear them down over millions of years.

Old mountain

A young mountain is jagged. As it gets older, the elements slowly wear it down and it becomes more rounded.

e sculptures

As a glacier creeps along,
it scrapes at the mountainside.
Eventually it gouges out huge,
U-shaped valleys, such as this
one in California, USA.

Rolling rocks

Ice breaks away small
rocks from the mountain.
These tumble down the
slope and gather in
a heap at the bottom.

Plucky plants

Plants that grow high up on the mountain slopes have adapted to cope with the biting cold, fierce winds and freezing weather there.

Tiny trees
Some willow and birch trees grow high up the mountainside. They avoid the howling winds by hugging the ground.

Alpine snowbell

The alpine snowbell gives off heat, which melts the snow around it. The plant's heat enables it to bloom in spring.

Growing on rocks

Lichens live on rocky peaks. They make acids that make the rocks crumble. Then they send tiny roots into the rocks to suck up any goodness in them.

Adaptable animals

Some animals that live on mountains have adapted to cope with the steep slopes. Others have adapted to living with high winds and freezing conditions.

Hot bath

Japanese macaque monkeys wallow in hot pools during the cold winters. The water is heated by volcanoes.

Mountain climber

Mountain goats are good at scrabbling over the rocky mountain faces. Their hooves are hollow and act like suction pads, helping the goats to grip.

Natural anti-freeze

The Yarrow's spiny lizard's blood stays liquid in temperatures below freezing, so it can survive on icy peaks in Mexico.

Living on mountains

Mountain peoples have learned to live in steep, remote and sometimes dangerous places. They grow crops for food and raise animals there.

Mountain animals

Yaks are useful animals. They provide farmers with food and wool. They are also used to carry goods.

Mountain cities

Kathmandu nestles in the Himalayas. It has the same facilities as any other modern city.

Growing food

Mountain fields are steep and there is not much soil. Many farmers build terraces to stop the soil washing away.

Going places

It can be difficult to travel on mountains because they are very steep. People have come up with clever ways for making mountain travel easier.

Long and winding roads

Mountain roads do not follow a straight line because they would be too steep to climb. The roads take a zigzagging route instead.

Climbing on a cable

A moving cable pulls this cable car between stations at the top and bottom of a mountain. Skiers use cable cars to get to snow high up on mountains.

Tourism

Mountains are great places to explore and enjoy. People can ski, trek, climb or mountain bike along the steep slopes. But we must protect these places so that everyone can enjoy them in the future.

Jumping off

Hang-gliders jump off mountain tops to float down on their wings. They glide on the warm air that rises from the ground.

Winter sports

Skiers and snowboarders love snow-covered mountains. They can slide and jump down the slippery slopes.

Mountain of rubbish

Many tourists drop their rubbish on mountain visits. This pollutes the area and can harm the wildlife that lives there.

Mountain resources

Hidden inside mountains lie valuable resources, such as building materials and metals. There are also useful resources on the slopes, such as trees.

Building blocks

Each day, big dumper trucks remove tonnes of rock and rubble from mountains. It is used to make buildings and bridges.

Cutting down trees

Logging companies plant fast-growing trees on mountainsides. When the trees are grown, loggers cut them down for timber and fuel.

Mining metal

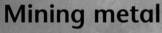

Some mountain rocks are rich in gold, silver, copper and tin. Miners use large drills to dig these metals out of the stone.

Mountaineering today

Today's mountaineers are well prepared for their climbs. They have special food for energy, layers of clothing for warmth and lots of safety equipment.

A good night's rest
Mountaineers shelter in tents at night and in bad weather. The tents are light to carry, strong and waterproof.

Oxygen supply
Climbers carry tanks of oxygen, which they use to help them to breathe more easily in the thin mountain air.

imbing suit
Climbers wear one-piece suits filled with down for warmth. The suit is windproof and waterproof.

Reaching the top

Mountain climbing is a popular sport. Many people have now climbed even the highest mountains, including the tallest on land, Mount Everest.

George Mallory

Andrew Irvine

Last climb

Mallory and Irvine began to climb Everest in 1924. Both men died on the mountain, but no one knows if they reached the top before they died.

Extraordinary climber

Reinhold Messner has climbed the world's 14 highest peaks. He was the first person to climb Everest without extra oxygen.

Wonder woman
Catherine Destivelle is a world-class climber. She tackles dangerous slopes and often uses only one or two of her fingers to pull herself upwards.

Avalanche!

A large mass of snow and ice can suddenly break loose and crash down a mountainside. This is called an avalanche.

Predicting avalanches

Scientists use information gathered in weather stations like this one to help them predict when avalanches are likely.

Avalanche in action

Some avalanches move as fast as a racing car. They sweep away everything in their path, including trees, people and even villages.

Protection

This steel fence has been built to stop an avalanche from reaching the town further downhill. It will slow down an avalanche.

Mountain **rescue**

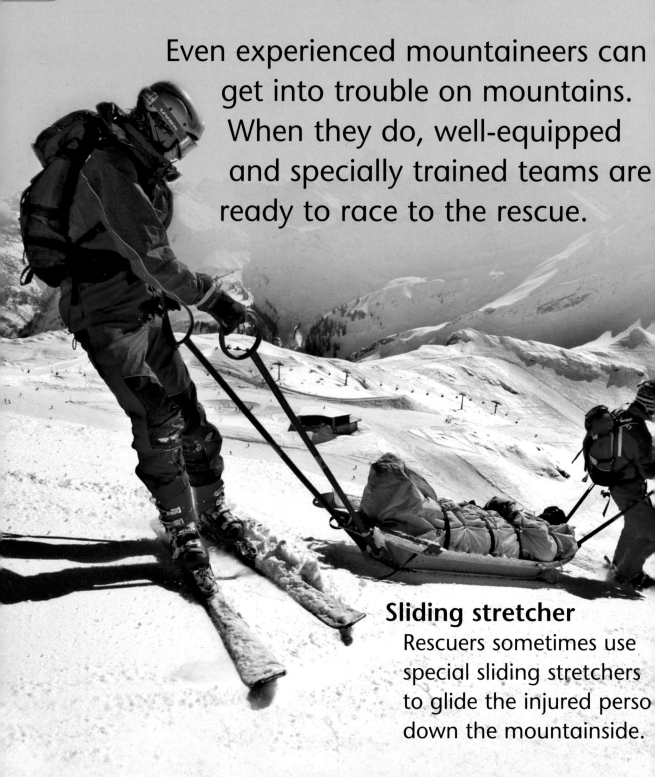

Even experienced mountaineers can get into trouble on mountains. When they do, well-equipped and specially trained teams are ready to race to the rescue.

Sliding stretcher
Rescuers sometimes use special sliding stretchers to glide the injured perso down the mountainside.

elicopter rescue
Helicopters can reach
remote peaks quickly.
Rescuers can then help
the injured people and
take them to hospital.

Rescue dog
St Bernard dogs have a strong
sense of smell. They can be
specially trained to sniff out
the victims of avalanches.

Mountain mysteries

People sometimes see some strange things when they climb a mountain. They might find fossil fish, or they might be followed by a huge shadow.

Ghostly shadow

If someone climbs a mountain when the Sun is low, the Sun casts an enormous shadow on any low clouds.

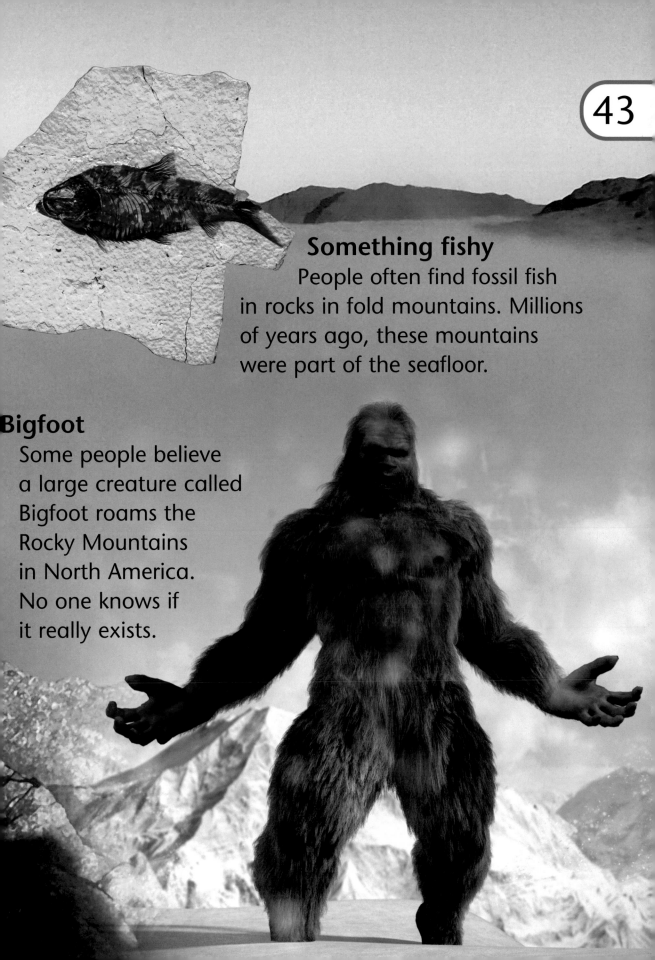

Something fishy

People often find fossil fish in rocks in fold mountains. Millions of years ago, these mountains were part of the seafloor.

Bigfoot

Some people believe a large creature called Bigfoot roams the Rocky Mountains in North America. No one knows if it really exists.

Making mountains

Make a fold mountain range
Discover how land is forced upwards when two plates collide by doing this simple experiment.

Roll out each ball of clay to make a rough square 25mm thick.

You will need
- 2 balls of modelling clay, different colours
- Tray
- Rolling pin
- Plastic food wrap

Lay both pieces 10mm apart on the plastic food wrap on the tray.

Gently push the two clay blocks together. Your mountain range will rise upwards.

Leaving footprints

Bigfoot's calling card

Bigfoot's footprints are called its 'calling card'. Make one to give to a friend.

You will need
- Large sheet of card
- Paints and paintbrush
- Marker pen or felt-tip pen
- Scissors
- Sponge

Fold the card in half, then paint a big foot shape. Cut out the shape, but do not cut the folded side.

On a sponge, draw a smaller foot shape. Cut this out.

Dip the sponge in some paint and decorate your card with lots of little footprints walking up towards the toes.

Your giant calling card is ready. Write a message inside.

Moving cable car

Make a cable car

Cable cars can climb high mountains on moving cables. Make a model with stations at the top and bottom of your mountain range.

You will need

- 3 small cereal boxes
- Coloured paper
- Sharp pencil
- Modelling clay
- 1 long, 1 short piece of string
- Marbles
- Sticky tape
- 1 small sweet box

1

Cover the cereal boxes with coloured paper. Decorate with shapes of mountains and trees.

2

Pierce a hole in the top of each box with a sharp pencil. Use modelling clay to push against.

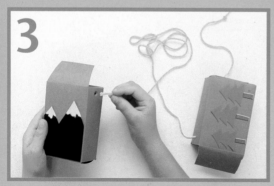

3

Thread the long piece of string through the holes as shown.

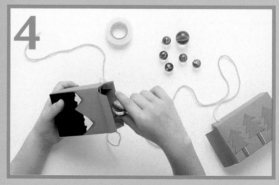

4

Place some marbles in each box, then tape the boxes shut.

5

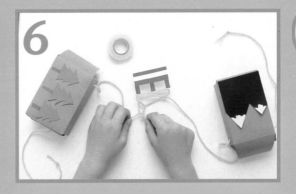

6

Decorate the small sweet box with coloured paper to make it look like a cable car.

Tape the short piece of string to the car, then tie it to the middle of the long piece of string.

Place the top station on a box. By pulling on the long piece of string, you can move your cable car from the station at the bottom, up the mountain to the station at the top.

Glossary

Acids – substances that can eat away other substances

Adapted – changed over time

Air – the mixture of gases that we breathe

Buckle – to crumple and fold

Cable – a long, thick rope usually made from metal wire

Conifer – an evergreen tree that keeps its leaves all year round

Crust – the hard, rocky surface of the Earth

Deciduous tree – a tree that loses its leaves in autumn

Down – soft, hair-like feathers that cover young birds

Earthquake – shaking of the ground caused by a sudden movement in the Earth's crust

Elements – strong winds, heavy rain and other kinds of bad weather

Erupt – to explode, throwing ash, gas and hot rocks into the air

Experienced – describes people who have skill which they have gained over time

Facilities – buildings and services, such as health care and schools

Fossil – the remains of ancient animals or plants found in rock

Fuel – a substance burnt to produce heat or power

Glide – to move smoothly and quietly

Gouge – to make a hole in something with force

Hollow – a shallow hole

Jagged – describes a surface that sharp and uneven

Lichen – a slow-growing plant the forms crusty branches on rocks, walls and trees

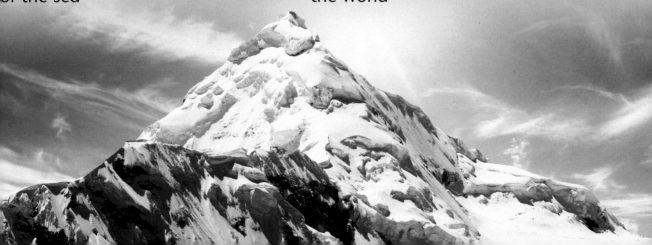

ygen – a common gas in the air
that is necessary for human life

ak – the top part of a mountain

tes – large areas of land
that 'float' on the liquid
rock underneath

llute – to make harmful waste
that damages the environment

edict – to say what will happen
in the future

y – a beam of light that travels
in a straight line

flect – to bounce back from
a surface

mote – describes out-of-the-
way places

sources – raw materials that can
be used to make other things

bble – a mixture of stones and
rocks of different sizes

afloor – the land at the bottom
of the sea

Steel – a strong metal made from
iron and carbon

Suction – the process that occurs
when two surfaces stick together
because the air between them
has been removed

Terraces – fields with steps going
down a hillside

Vegetation – plant life

World-class – among the best in
the world

This book includes material that would be particularly useful in helping to teach children aged 7–11. It covers many elements of the English and Science curricula and provides opportunities for cross-curricular lessons, especially those involving Geography and Art.

Extension activities

Writing
Read about Mallory and Irvine on page 36. Imagine what happened to them as they climbed Everest, and write it as a set of diary entries. Say if you think they reached the top or not before they died.

Read about the ghostly shadows on page 42, and write a poem describing your shadow as you climb a mountain.

Speaking and listening
Imagine you are reporter witnessing a volcanic eruption. Describe what you see.

Science
Background information is provided on the scientific themes of rocks (pp19, 20–21, 32–33), Earth (pp6–7, 8–9, 10–11, 12–13 habitats (pp14–15, 22–23, 24–25 26–27) and forces (pp29, 30–31, 38–39, 40).

Find some different types of rock near where you live. Compare them: do they look or feel different? Do they float or sink? D they soak up water? Are they har or soft? How heavy are they? Car you see grains in them? Are any magnetic? Display your findings in a chart.

How is the air different higher up a mountain? Write a short report describing how this affects people Pages 7, 17 and 35 will help you with your research.

Read pages 10–11. Make your own volcano by putting some baking soda (sodium bicarbonate into a container and pouring in vinegar (acetic acid), then watch the eruption. Use your craft skills to make the volcano look even more realistic.

oss-curricular links

ography: Find ten mountain
nges in an atlas, and make a
. showing which countries they
e in. Try to find out the name
 the highest mountain in each
nge as well.

hat is the nearest mountain to
ere you live? Is it young or old?
w do you think it was formed?
e pages 20–21 to help you.

t: Look at the picture on page
. Make a collage of a mountain
ene where only one side is rainy.
n you make your collage 3-D?

t/design/geography: Can you
ake a terraced mountain? You
ll need to cut the outline of a
ountain as seen from above
to cardboard. Then cut slightly
aller outlines and glue each
yer on top. You will slowly build
terraced mountain.

Using the projects
Children can follow or adapt these
projects at home. Here are some
ideas for extending them:

Page 44: Form the modelling clay
into two cylinder shapes and push
them together. What happens if
you pull them apart at the ends?

Page 45: Make a footprint in a tray
of soil or sand. Pour plaster mixed
with water into it so it is covered.
When the plaster is set, lift up your
'fossilized' footprint.

Page 46–47: Can you create a
mountain landscape for your
cable car?

Did you know?

- Some mountain ranges are older than others. The Highlands in Scotland are 400 million years old, while the Alps in central Europe are only 15 million years old.

- The longest mountain range in the world is the Andes in South America. The mountains stretch for over 7,000 kilometres.

- The slam of a car door, a falling branch or the movement of a skier can all start an avalanche. Snow can speed down a mountain at 320 kilometres per hour!

- Glaciers store about 70 per cent of the world's supply of fresh water and cover about 10 per cent of the Earth's land.

- At the top of the Himalayas, fierce winds can reach more than 300 kilometres per hour.

- The highest altitude at which trees will grow is called the tree line. The highest tree line in the world is in the Bolivian Andes, where hardy trees can grow up to 5,200 metres above sea level.

- K2 is the second highest mounta on Earth after Everest. It is know as the 'Savage Mountain'. One i five people that have tried to reach the top have died. Only 30 people have ever made it to the summit, compared to the 2,700 that have scaled Everest. K2 has never been climbed in winter.

- Measured from the base, the tallest mountain is not Everest bu Hawaii's Mauna Kea, which rises to a height of 9,500 metres from the seafloor.

- Because the temperature at the top of a mountain is much colde than at the bottom, it is possible to have snow at the equator, the warmest part of the world.

The Himalayan jumping spider lives higher up than any other animal. At around 6,700 metres, its only food is insects blown by the wind from lower levels.

The plates that folded up to form the Himalayas are still crashing into each other. Some mountains, such as Everest, continue to grow higher by about a centimetre each year!

Mount Stromboli, on a small Italian island, is one of the world's most active volcanoes. It has been erupting almost non-stop for the past 20,000 years!

- Mountain people and animals can live at great heights because they have bigger hearts and lungs, which carry more blood and oxygen.

- The world's highest ever cable car system was located in the city of Mérida in Venezuela. It was over 12 kilometres long and reached a height of nearly 4,800 metres.

- Tourism brings a lot of money for the people who live in the mountains. The Alps receives about 100 million visitors every year.

Mountains quiz

The answers to these questions can all be found by looking back through the book. See how many you get right. You can check your answers on page 56.

1) Which mountain range is home to the world's highest peaks?
A – Andes
B – Himalayas
C – Alps

2) When do mountains form?
A – When two plates push against each other
B – When two plates stay still
C – When two plates move away from each other

3) Where is air the thinnest in the mountains?
A – Down in the valleys
B – At the tops
C – Among the pine trees

4) What is a large crack in a glacier called?
A – Lammergeier
B – Crevasse
C – Cirque

5) Which of these does not make rocks crumble?
A – Sunlight
B – Lichens
C – Glaciers

6) Why do farmers build terraces?
A – To separate different crops
B – To attract tourists
C – To stop the soil washing away

7) Which of these is used to get up a mountain?
A – Cable car
B – Hang-glider
C – Snowboard

8) What valuable material can be found in mountains?
A – Glass
B – Plastic
C – Metal

9) Reinhold Messner was the first person to climb Everest without...
A – A tent
B – Extra oxygen
C – Food

10) What breed of dog is used to sniff ou the victims of avalanches?
A – Jack Russell
B – St Bernard
C – Pug

11) Which can move downhill the quickest?
A – A glacier
B – An avalanche
C – A skier

12) Where is Bigfoot believed to live?
A – Kathmandu
B – Hawaiian islands
C – Rocky Mountains

oks to read

th's Shifting Surface (Sci-Hi) by Robert *inedden, Heinemann Library, 2010*

onder Why Mountains Have Snow On Top by Jackie Gaff, Kingfisher, 2012

Cycles: Mountain by Sean Callery, *Kingfisher, 2012*

Mountain Environment (Step-up Geography) by Clare Hibbert, Evans *Brothers, 2005*

untain Food Chains (Protecting Food Chains) by Rachel Lynette, Heinemann *Library, 2011*

untains (Extreme Habitats) by Susie *Hodge, TickTock Books, 2007*

untains (Go Facts: Natural Environments) *by Ian Rohr, A&C Black, 2009*

ices to visit

vis Range, near Fort William, Scotland *w.nevisrange.co.uk* **i**rn about the wildlife, habitats and **i**dscape that surround Ben Nevis, the **i**hest mountain in the UK. Depending **i** the season, the resort offers a range **i**ctivities, from walking and mountain **i**ing to skiing and snowboarding. You **i** also enjoy a cable car ride up the **i**untain to a height of 650 metres.

owdon Mountain Railway, **i**rth Wales *w.snowdonrailway.co.uk* **i**e a railway trip to the very top of **i**owdon, the highest mountain in **i**les. The visitor centre at the top is the **i**hest building in England and Wales.

Highland Wildlife Park, Kincraig, Scotland
www.highlandwildlifepark.org
Discover some of the creatures that live in mountain habitats around the world in this spectacular wildlife park. Highlights include red pandas, Przewalski horses and Japanese macaques.

Websites

http://vulcan.wr.usgs.gov/Outreach/ AboutVolcanoes/framework.html
Why do volcanoes occur? When will a volcano erupt? How hot is a volcano? Find out the answers to these and other questions on this site.

http://primaryhomeworkhelp.co.uk/ mountains/types.htm
On this site for primary school children find out how different types of mountains are formed.

www.onegeology.org/eXtra/kids/ earthProcesses/glaciers.html
This website lets you explore Earth's processes. You can find out all about glaciers, including how they form, how they move and how they melt.

Mountains quiz answers

1) B   7) A
2) A   8) C
3) B   9) B
4) B   10) B
5) A   11) B
6) C   12) C